This book is dedicated to all of the growing-up people of the world but very specially to: the Sithole Kids - Joseph, Keikanne, Godson Tendai; the Tynes Kids - Corey, Timothy, Sophia, Shelley, Stephanie, Haiti, Little Max; the Thomas Kids - Angela, Georgie; the Nyajeka Kids - Tandi, Shingai; and to Goddaughter Kathleen Graham and her sister Christine. Always be good to the Earth and to your families and to each other.

Save the World for Me

Maxine Tynes

Pottersfield Press
Lawrencetown Beach

Canadian Cataloguing in Publication Data
  Tynes, Maxine
  Save the world for me
  ISBN 0-919001-70-X

I. Title
PS8589.Y54S28 1991   jC811'.54   C91-097624-4
PZ7.T96Sa 1991

Cover photograph: Lesley Choyce

Author photo: Shirley Robb

Inside illustrations by Maxine Tynes

This book was produced with the financial assistance of Multiculturalism Canada - The Secretary of State for Multiculturalism and
Citizenship.

Pottersfield Press receives block grant funding from The Canada
Council and the Nova Scotia Department of Tourism and Culture.

Reprinted in 1995 thanks to the support of the Multicultural
Programs of the Department of Canadian Heritage.

Printed in Canada on recycled paper

Pottersfield Press
Lawrencetown Beach
RR 2, Porters Lake, Nova Scotia
Canada BOJ 2S0

Contents

Your World

I'm a Kid of the World

I am one of the kids of the world,
a kid of the world that's free.
I'm not too big or tall or small—
my part of the world just nicely fits me.

Sometimes I lie about in the sun
sometimes I hang out in trees
sometimes I'm just so full of beans
my energy zips me around like the breeze.

I'm one of the kids you might see on your block
on your street or down a dirt road.
When I'm alone I explore and I'm quiet
but when we're a bunch
we shout and we laugh like a riot.

I'm a kid of the world
and I like it just fine.
If you take care of it now
someday its care will be mine.

Arachnid My Love

Spiders in the bathroom
spiders on your nose
spiders in the garden
sliding down a hose.

I used to get the willies
whenever they came near—
those fat and skinny spiders
with eight legs everywhere.

And then I learned about them
and how they eat their webs—
they suck their toes
they munch mosquitoes
and then they begin to spin again.

In lots of ways they help us
eating insects that cause trouble—
the next arachnid that you see
don't squash him
he deserves a spidery hug
or a present of a gift-wrapped gourmet bug.

Mum Calls Me a Mall Crawler

Mum calls me a mall crawler
she says the mall's my fun
she says she never sees me—
when I hear the words "the mall" I run

Don't know what's new on sale there
don't care what's been marked down
my friends and me we just hang out
in this air conditioned indoor town

Some store folks call us "mall-rats"
some shoppers sneer and frown
they cringe when they see a bunch of us
we herd together
we roam around

We love to dress outrageously
in hats and holey tights
and roller blades and mini skirts
and rappers' pants
and hair chopped and shaved and neon bright

My mum says we are mall crawlers
we just roam the mall so free
so any mall you go to
that kid inside might just be me.

Prism Rainbows in the Light

Rainbows, rainbows on my wall
a garden of rainbows over all
some are short, some dart about
some are long and bright and float
spears of violet, red and blue
dots of green and every hue
magic colour shadows splash my face
the wall, the floor and every place.

I call it magic just for fun
but my science teacher taught me
about refracted light
but words like "prism" and "suncatcher"
make me think of magic, magic, magic
magic colour shadows
rainbows on my wall
even when no rainbow's in the sky at all
standing in their colours
rainbows in my hair
I can swim in rainbow colours almost
everywhere.

When Someone Special Dies

My grandma died this weekend
and my granddad died last year.
I know they're gone
but in my head their smiles and voices are so clear.

I saw grandma just last week.
We all went to the mall
where she bought me neon shoelaces
and that poster on the wall.
We snacked on pop and pizza,
we found her shoes that were too small,
we talked to friends,
we shopped 'til we dropped
and on the bus ride home
we planned to do it again.

But now my grandma won't do that
or anything, ever again.
She died this weekend.
(Granddad died last year.)
I'm sad and confused
and don't know how I should feel
or what to say or what to do.

Mum's eyes are red. Dad blows his nose.
They hug me hard.
They tell me that life ends, then begins again.
But Grandma and Granddad,
does that mean you, too?

Old Enough

Old enough to wear a key
around my neck at school, at play
old enough to be home alone
those hours when Mom or Dad's away
old enough to cook alone
to lock the doors
to talk and talk and talk on the phone
to question the look in a stranger's eye
to turn away from friends who smoke
or steal or drink or think drugs are a joke
old enough for so many things
but I still need my mom and dad
for a talk and a hug
for a zillion things more.

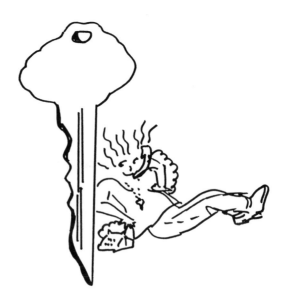

Pizza for Breakfast

Pizza for my breakfast
cereal for my lunch
toast and cheese for suppertime
my menu's all mixed up.

But that's the way it is these days
eating morning-things at night.
Who knows if pasta's on for lunch
tossed with fruit and tiger toes?
As long as it's edible
anything goes.

My Uncle Goes to Literacy School

My uncle goes to literacy school
and my mum helps him, too
his lessons are a bit like mine
with writing, spelling and punctuation rules.

My uncle's almost six feet tall
he tells me I'm tall too
but I know that's not all we share
we have homework and lessons
and books to read
lots to learn
we like doing it too.

I watched my uncle reading
his brow was furrowed tight
he worked with concentration
with a homework snack of apples near
sometimes he took a bite.

I asked my uncle why he tried
to study just like me
at first he thought, and then he said
"knowing how to read and write
makes me feel so strong
and able to do everything I need and want
to help me and my family along."

Home Is

Home is where you hang your hat
where you feed the cat
wipe your feet on the mat

Home is where you have your stuff
make some noise
play nice and play rough

Home is where you mess up your room
play music loud
dance to rap tunes

Home is where folks ought to be
at daylight and midnight
sometimes at noon, sometimes at three

Home is a place where relatives roam
where friends drop in
where you can whine, giggle, tease,
or sing an off-key song

Home is where families
can tell home truths and little fibs
can love, hug, bug, jostle, race,
pull hair, joke, wrestle, be happy, mad or sad
have dirty fingernails or clean
and always, always, after tears and fights
after did-not, did-so, push-me, pull-you,
topsy-turvy days
forgive and forget and be good friends
with each other

Home is.

Holiday in the City for Some

Well we don't go to cottages
and we don't play in boats
and we don't go to summer camp
and we don't travel about

We don't have money for all of that.
Mom says we make do—just that—no more.
We live in a house that the city owns—
they own the fridge;
they own the stove;
they even own my bedroom door.

So summer in the city is all I ever know.
There are parks and stuff
but not a cabin as far as the eye can see.

A lake's nearby
and the beach is, too
and in a big city like Quebec or Toronto
there's always the zoo.

I guess there's always something to do
like computers at the library
or soccer in the park
or videos maybe once a week
and a cookout or a sleepout in someone's yard
with a campfire after dark.

So I guess it's okay not going away
to some cottage by the lake
where you can't skateboard with frogs
or deliver papers as a summer job
like you can if you're home in the city
all summer long.

A Best and Furry Secret Friend

I still sleep with my Teddy bear
no one's supposed to know
not the kids that I skateboard with
or go to scary movies with;
or, you know, just hang out.

'Cause Teddy's my secret night-time friend
he's always there for me
he doesn't care if I'm mad or sad
or feeling crazy or lazy
'cause that's sometimes the way I am.

Old Teddy's always there for me
as a pillow or a friend
he never complains if I hog all the bed
or in the middle of the night if I drool
or cry or cough on his head.

This Teddy is soft when I pull his ears
in the middle of the night-time snooze
when my eyes are closed
and my toes are cold
he's still my night-time friend
with no complaints when I put out the lights.

Now if I was two or three or four
this would be all right
Mom or Dad would tuck me in
with Teddy in plain sight.

But now I'm eight or ten years old
or twelve or even more
with torn out air-holes in my jeans
with New Kids or Hammer posters on my door

my clothes and stuff cover my floor
(Mom says I raise fungus in the mess behind
my closet door).

So night-time is the only time
I bring my Teddy out
I dig through the clutter
with my earphones on
and pull him from the floor.

He's old and soft and floppy now
from years of being hugged
he still gets that—a hug from me
and I guess that's more than just okay
this secret friendship—old Teddy and me.

Privacy

This thing called privacy
so invisible and so important
it has no colour
no size
no shape to its name
but you carry it with you
it's almost a game.
How much of you will you share and show
and when is it o.k. to touch
and when is it not?

There's body privacy
when you say "No" to
invasion of your personal self

not to a pinch on the cheek
or a pat on the back
or a bear hug
or a round the shoulders "Well-done!" teacher hug

but the kind of body privacy for you alone
for bathing
for dressing
for your eyes and for doctors' eyes
and for stay-well touching only.

Privacy.
So peculiar and precious to us all.
We want it.
We demand it.
We guard it, sometimes with room signs that
say:
DO NOT DISTURB!

PLEASE KNOCK!
PRIVATE! KEEP OUT!
THIS MEANS YOU!

This thing called privacy.
It puzzles and it pleases me
all at the same time.
It is mine.

Mama Drives a Taxi

Mama drives a taxi
Dad sees me off to school
my family lives in the 1990s
there are some old and some new family rules.

When my Mum was a little girl
women worked all day at home
while dads left home in early morn
for office, truck, school or store.

But now in the 1990s
kids and mums and dads
live many different family ways.

In my house that's okay
for my stay-home Dad
my taxi Mum
and me!

The Greeny, Meany Grouchies

I'm in a meany, greeny mood
feeling all bad; never good
'cause the greeny, meany grouchies are here again.

And the greeny, meany grouchies
take my smiles and leave a frown
and though I try and try and try
my mouth turns down and down and down.

I look mad
and I act bad
my Please and Thank-you are gone
and I make noise
and I yell hard
and I stomp and pound and roar.

I push and I pull
my sister's hair
I take my brother's stuff
'cause the greeny, meany grouchies
are making me act rough.

Won't eat my food
won't find my socks
won't brush my teeth
won't stop to talk
won't feed the dog
won't pat the cat
won't make my bed
won't sit on anybody's lap.

But when a big hug finds me
when family arms fold me up and hold me close
the greeny, meany grouchies disappear
leaving me with my old smile back again.

Skateboard Skatedown

I'm zipping
and I'm flying
and I'm popping off the curb
I am greased lightning down a hillside
gaining airspeed like a bird

My hair's slicked back by the air-flow
my t-shirt's flapping in the breeze
I'm a speedy skateboard rider
I'm a rider on the breeze

I wear air-conditioned blue-jeans
so my knees poke through the holes
shoelaces fly out from my runners
quicksilver fuels my toes

I need kneepads for this madness
and a bike crash helmet, too
I'm a breathless skateboard rider
look out world, I'm flying through!

Is It Okay to Look?

Is it okay for me to look at you
as you go limping down the street?
May I look at your wheelchair?
May I pick up your cane?
May I watch how you get up the stairs
that I can run up and down as easy as rain?
My mom tells me not to look
at your twisted lips or legs or arms or hands
but I want to see
and to ask you, too—
What's it like?
Does it hurt?
Could it happen to me?
How'd it happen to you?
I'm not sure that I should look at you,
not sure just what to say or do
'cause my body is whole and normally strong.
Your body is different.
I'm me.
You are you.
I finally do take a chance—
I look at you, you look back
and then you smile.

24

The "No" Word

The NO word is for:
 ...friends who are not friends who say,
 "Come on. Let's take that," in a store
when they think no one is watching!

The NO word is for:
 ...friends who are not friends who say,
 "Come on. Let's see what smoking is like."

The NO word is for:
 ...friends who are not friends who say:
 "Come on. Your mom or dad or granny
will never miss that money. Take it!"

The NO word is for:
 ...friends who are not friends who say,
 "Come on. It won't hurt you. Try it.
I do it all the time."
Trying to get you to do the D-word, drugs.

The NO word is for:
 ...friends who are not friends who say,
 "Come on. Let me in your house after school.
Your parents will never know."

The NO word is for:
 ...friends who are not friends
 who say bad words,
 who poke fun at people
who look different than you do,
 who talk different than you do,
 who walk different than you do,
or who are different in some way.

The NO word is for:
    a touch that is wrong,
    a touch that feels funny,
    a touch under your clothes,
    a touch that feels bad,
    a touch that you are not allowed to tell about,
or a touch that hurts!

The NO word is a special word.
It's a strong word, too.
It's good to use when the time is wrong
          when the words are wrong
          when the doing
              doing
              doing is wrong
and when you know you want to be strong.
Use the NO word.
Say it **LOUD** and say it **STRONG**!

The NO word has muscles for your heart
and for your mind
And for your SAFETY, too!
So say it!
Say the NO word!
Be safe!
Be strong!
Be a NO word person!
Be proud of you!
Altogether now.
LOUD and STRONG!
Make that voice big!
Let it go!
NO!

School World

The Trick of the Clock

Books are flying everywhere,
pencils are on the floor.
They turn themselves into roller skates
as I head out the door.

Where is my key?
Is that my lunch?
My project's missing too.
I've missed the bus—
it's been here and gone
Oh, what am I to do?

That old alarm clock by my bed
is playing tricks again;
it starts to wake me up on time
then makes me go to sleep again.

It happens every Monday
or any school day of the week.
It makes me snooze.
It makes me late.
Then while I'm dressing up for school
my socks play hide and seek

No time to wash behind my ears,
just time to catch the neighbours' car
with kids like me
with a clock like mine
playing alarm clock tricks
with school morning time.

Stop Eating Those Poems!

Stop eating those poems!
Save some for me—
I like mine with mustard
I like mine with cheese
spread with jam
or crisp like toast
or baked and browned like a great big roast
stuffed with garlic
stuffed with herbs
like thyme and basil
rosemary and gazurb

Who knows what gazurb is?
Who cares if it tastes so good?
Just make sure you have lots of it
on the make-a-poem-sandwich assembly line.

The Teacher Who Sees All and Hears All and Knows All

It's one o'clock
and time for English, or math.
My teacher's footstep is in the hall—
that hand is on the door,
that teacher's head pokes through the door
as the voice says, "Open books.
Go to the board.
Do question four. Then do questions 6 to 24."

That eye is looking right through me.
It sees me fidget and sneak some early lunch
and make faces at my friends
and whisper and talk.
That teacher eye compares my work to all the rest.
It sees me enter class late again.

My teacher sees all that I do
and knows all things about me
like that I'm weak in some things
but I'm strong in math, computers, too
and that coaxing is what I need
to get my projects done on time,
to do all assignments,
to study well, to clearly write
to use all classtime, all the time.

It's one o'clock
and time for English, art or math.
My teacher's here.
But where am I,
where is my mind?
I guess we both will see.
It's not that I don't like school
or doing all the work.
It's just that I have a teacher
who sees all and hears all, too.
No goofing off for me, I guess
when my teacher is in view!

Computer Fantasy

Computers make me have a wish
that I was very small
so small that I could sit on the ENTER key
and slip with a beep so deep inside
into the world of bits and bytes and
microchips and database
to see what's going on.

Maybe I'd be the cursor on your screen
and just go blinking by
don't delete me as I'm having fun
press down on any old alphabet key
turn me into a letter or
an X that multiplies and fills up the screen
then print me out
give me a hard copy ride.

Computers make me have a wish
to do all kinds of things
to write as fast as I can think
to play word games or do graphics on screen
and of course I can do all of that
'cause computers are so neat
they're fast, they're here, they're everywhere
making fun and homework a speedy breeze.

But my dream is to shrink and to get inside
to see how a circuit board works
to see that micro-memory
in the motherboard where it lurks and works
to taste the brains of microchips
to see Lotus 1, 2, 3 —
it's just a dream as the cursor blinks
my computer fantasy.

You're Not My Favourite Teacher

I don't like you Mr. Something.
Ms. Blank you bug me too
each day in class I want to chat
but you always say, "There's work to do."

I wiggle and waggle in my seat—
you make me stop that too.
I get wonderful "What if" ideas in math
but you say that's for language arts
and to stick to the numbers
to get back on track.

You never see my hand up
when it flaps up in the air
I know that verb
I know that date
I know that history why and where.

But the only thing you say to me
in every class all day
is "It's messy. Please do that again."
"No talking. This is not time for play."

I don't like you Mr. Something
Ms. Blank you bug me too
I think you think up nasty things
for me and all my friends to do.

Dear Mr. Premier, and
Mr. Minister of Education,
This Is a Test

Do you know what it's like to be me?
Do you know that I'm in Grade 7 or 10 in Digby?
In Primary in Weymouth or Yarmouth?
That I'm in Grade 11 or 12 in Sydney or Dartmouth
or Truro or in Preston?
That I'm headed off to trade school
or French Immersion or to college?
Will you help me to get there?
Will you let me keep my gym class?
My art class? My French class?
Will you cut my class of 40 in half so I can breathe?
So my teacher can get to my desk
when I need help?
So my teacher will know my name
when I raise my hand?
Will you let my teacher teach me?
Will you give us the books and buses that we need?
Will you put the history and literature
of Native People and
of Black People and of Acadians
centre stage in our textbooks
And in our classrooms where they belong?

Mr. Premier,
Mr. Minister of Education, this is a test.

Do our parents' tax dollars feed you well?
Have you eaten from a food bank?
Have you been saved by a women's shelter?

Mr. Premier,
Mr. Minister of Education, this is a test.

If you pass, *my* future is secure.
If you fail, *your* kids go to private school,
but I don't learn to learn.
My school door starts to close.

This First Day of September

This first day of September
this sad-filled happy golden
September day.
The memory of August heat lingers,
and is gone;
the memory of all those golden leaves
of childhood's autumns, come and gone;
the ghost of little girl legs
one knee sock up,
one crinkled down
swishing through leaves
leaves
leaves
finding acorns and horse chestnuts
biting sour through green prickles
licking the brown silk nut-shine
hoarding horse chestnut bulges
in pocket, pocket, pocket—
swishing,
red, brown, gold-gold oak maple leaves
swishing, crunching, crackling
under these September feet.
All my red-gold sad and happy memories
this sad-filled happy golden September day.

Inuktitut's a Language

Inuktitut's a language
like French or English,
Hebrew, Italian, Lebanese,
Urdu, Welsh, Gaelic, Shona,
lots of others, too.
But I like this word Inuktitut

Inuktitut
Inuktitut
How do you speak Inuktitut?
How do you say It's raining?
             I'm too hot?
             I love you?
             Pass the bread?
But even in Inuktitut I don't want to hear
It's time for bed.

Watcher of the World

To be a watcher of the world
to grab a headline on the run
to know the name of Mr. This-or-That
and all that he has done
to keep apartheid alive
or to tax the people poor.
Be a watcher of the world.
It's what you can do, and more.

To be a watcher of the world
in your own country's back yard, too.
To know that our country's ailing
it has the *we-don't-know-who-we-are flu*!
There's only one cure for the virus
And that one cure is you
Be a watcher of Canada.
Steer your folks right on election day.

Be a watcher of the world
in your home, school, community, too.
Help folks "butt out."
Clean up the streets.
Recycling's cool, and a life-saver, too!

Keep a close eye on racism, sexism
and child abuse, too.
In ten years or less you can
vote it out, work it out
stamp it out, shout it out!

This is your world.
Watch what we and you can do.

This Canada

Tell me what this country is
this Canada
this nation of same and different
>of faces and voices and places and trees
>of east and west
>of Inuit, Aboriginal
>of French and English
>and everyone else in between.

Tell me what this country feels
this Canada
this nation of together and separate
>of push and pull
>of *bonjour* and good morning
>of stars and stripes becoming
>of northern lights showing tears
>of the first people.

Show me a map of this country
this Canada
charted with a past that beckons and keeps us
charted with rivers of hopes and dreams
shaped by winds of change
shaded with the faces of you and of us
as we move toward new freedoms
as we come into our own
This Canada.

What Can I Do for the World Today?

What can I do for the world, today?
I can spread the news
to reduce
to recycle
and re-use.

What can I do for the world today?
I can re-sole, re-use
repair my shoes.

What can I do for the world today?
Start a green-thumb club,
build a backyard compost,
then when you boil an egg or eat an orange
toss in the peel and stuff.

What can I do for the world today?
Not litter.
Not waste.
Not destroy marshlands and tidepools.

What can I do for the world today?
Lots!
What can you do?

Big World

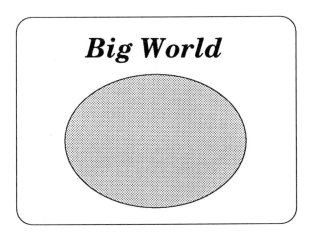

Save the World for Me

Save the world for me
save a lake for me to fish in,
a pond for me to swim in
a stream to wade in
fresh water, clean in wells
and in drinking glasses.

Save the world for me
save the Great Lakes
and Halifax Harbour
save the air to breathe
over Winnipeg and Vancouver
over Toronto, Inuvik, Montreal, St. John's
and everywhere.

Keep the Bay of Fundy blue
and the Arctic tundra white
keep the Annapolis Valley green
and my peas and carrots fresh and
healthy like they're supposed to be
keep my milk sweet and clean.

Save the world for me
save it from landfills
and from Chernobyl
and from nuclear weaponry.

Save the world for me.

What and How and Why?

Why do some bad things happen?
Why do some kids hurt and cry?
Why are some people homeless?
Why do some birds no longer fly?

Why do disasters happen?
Why are there wars and floods?
Why do some homes go up in flames?
What kills the trees?
Who is to blame?

Why are some kids hurt badly?
Why do some families split?
Why is the news so full of hate
and theft and things that devastate?

Where are all the answers?
Who can answer all my whys?
I think my answers can be found
in hearts and homes and people's eyes.

Remember for each sad time
for each unanswered why
there is a warm and friendly hand
to help, to play, to fix
to point to a rainbow in the sky
to join other hands in a circle
to always be there
as a friend for a friend.

Amputee Ecology

Some of us have lost a foot
some have one leg gone
sometimes a hand's no longer there
sometimes an arm was there then gone
sometimes a finger or a toe
sometimes two or more are lost.

Maybe we sit much better than we run
sometimes a hop is traded for a walk
sometimes a toothbrush
is held tight with the toes
sometimes a toe reaches up to scratch a nose
armless kids comb their own hair too
when legs twist up like pretzels
to reach high up to the head
or to reach for gooey pizza
or marshmallows toasted on the fire
or to slap at a mosquito
who is feasting on my hide.

When I Look at the Ocean

When I look at the ocean
When I look up at the sky
My own self seems so very small
It makes me wonder why
And wonder what part I am
In this great big universe, or world
Of planet Earth.

My feet are small
My hands are, too.
And I can't fly like birds.
But I can help keep green things green
And water clear and sweet
By picking up
And packing up
All garbage, trash and things
And by only buying what is good
For animals and for the land.

There's this word called E C O L O G Y
E N V I R O N M E N T is one, too.
Both mean the earth
            the sea
            the sky
But they also mean me and you.

When Black and White See Eye to Eye

When Black and White see eye-to-eye
Good times go round and round
But when they don't
Some push, some shout
Some fight; all stand and frown.

See eye-to-eye, I always say
See hand-to-hand
See heart-to-heart
See mind to mind to mind
Then Black meets White
Meets Brown meets Tan
Meets French meets Micmac
Meets Arab meets Jew
When Black and White sees eye-to-eye
This world fits and pleases me and you.

Yikes! It's the Summertime Road Trip!

I'm waking up, it's hot
I'm covered with road maps
there's an elbow in my eye
and someone's stinky sneaker is by my face
my eyes fly open
I see cows, trees, scenery speeding by.
Yikes! It's the summertime family road trip
one more time!

I guess I really like it
well, I know I really do
but it gets so hot and sticky
with four in the back seat
when it's only made for two.

There is me
my little brother
and my sister taking space
there's the dog who saw us packing
and got that "take me" look on his face.

The car is stuffed with twice its weight
sandwiches are squashed on the floor
the dash is stuffed with travel maps,
first aid kit, how to camping guide
and the keys to Uncle Harry's country cabin door.

We wrestle for the window seats
we yell for pop and treats
as neon signs roll by
we eat and drink and sing and fight
and squash more sandwiches with our feet.

Dad or Mom stops a kazillion times
for bathroom parades over and over again
and around every bend we yell:
ARE WE THERE YET?

While Mom and Dad just roll their eyes
the dog breathes doggie breath at us
and this overstuffed holiday car
keeps rolling, rolling on.

I Hurt/You Hurt

I hurt
you hit
you hit
I hurt
I hurt
I hit and hit and hit
friends hurt
they hit
they hit
I hurt
we hit
we hurt
and hurt
and hurt
and hurt
Why hit?
Why hurt?

I Am Old. I Am Old

I am old. I am old, my neighbour said
As he took a walk
As he stopped to talk.

I am old. I am old, my grandma said
As she fed her cat
As I sat on her lap.

I am old. I am old, my grandpa said
As he tied my shoes then picked up his harmonica
And played the blues.

I am old. I am old, my nana said
As she knitted my mittens
While we watched three little kittens.

I am old. I am old, my zayda said
As we munched on latkes
And we watched the snow fall
In the wintery darkness.

I am old. I am old, my bubba said
As we went shopping
She walking; me hopping.

I am old. I am old, Great Uncle said
As he tickled my chin
As he gave me a spin.

I am old. I am old, said all of these
As they work and play
Whether wrinkled, slow or grey
Doing and going and always loving
Day by day by day by day.

War Is Not Healthy for Children and for Other Living Things

War is scary
so big and far away for me
but nearby and noisy for a kid
somewhere else on the map.

But I can still play with my friends
and laugh and make silly words
and rude, rude sounds when I want to
like I sometimes do.

War is scary
so big and far away for me
but for some kid somewhere else on the map
the war is right next door.

I can turn off the TV
and the war is gone
but that kid crosses the street of war
on the way to school.

War is scary
but I can still sleep safe at night
and dream and wake up thinking
that maybe soon the world will be all right.

War is scary
but I can still wear my favourite colour
and eat a favourite treat
and sneak and do some bad-kid things.

In fact, I'm just like some kid somewhere
who knows what guns sound like up close.

But for kids like me war is only on my TV
like Nintendo
so I can turn it off
but some kids can't
because it's real
and right outside their door.

War is so scary
but I can get a smile sometimes
from my teacher
or a hug from my big sister or brother
from grammy or grandpa
or from Mom or Dad.

So can that other kid
the one far away on the map
where the war is
up close and loud and scary
where the war is so big
up close for her or him
so big but far away for me.

Someone Like You

Black or brown or white or tan
Big and fat and short and tall
Those who run fast
Those who fall
Those who tell fibs
Those who are true
Those with brothers, sisters, too!
Some with kitty-cats
Some with dogs
Someone has a fish - in - a - tank
Or a hamster, or a frog
Someone visits Mummy
Someone visits Dad
Some live with Mum and Dad
Just like that
Some no longer suck a thumb
Some have braces shiny
Some have a baby in the house
crying loud, but oh - so - tiny!
Some eat carrots
Some eat cake
Some like yogurt or pudding
Apple pie or kiwi too
All are people like me and like you.

I Have Three Legs, You Have Two

*This poem is for big and little people everywhere
who roll around in a wheelchair; or who thump
around with crutches or canes; or who bump around
with no legs; or who eat and comb their hair and
paint or work computers with their toes. And it's for
me and my cane, Stanley.*

I have three legs
You have two.
Three legs keep me standing
            standing
            standing
Three legs keep me standing
                on my feet!

When I go up stair-steps
            stair-steps
            stair-steps
When I go up stair-steps one-two-three
Three legs help me go up one-two-three.

When I do a hill climb
Not fast; S - L - O - W - L - Y
When I do a hill climb one-two-three
Three legs keep me standing
            standing
            standing
Three legs keep me standing on my feet!

The People Rainbow

When we open wide our eyes
when we look at each other
we see smiles and eyes and short
                              long
                    black, red, blonde, brown
                    and sometimes curly-curly hair

And we see faces like a rainbow all around
some are brown
and some are pink
and almost, almost white
(but not like snow)
some are like coffee
while some are golden, like wheat in a field

Black and brown and red and tan
all the colours of people
all the colours of the land

That's us
that's you,
and that's me too

We are colour.
We are the people rainbow.

Epilogue:

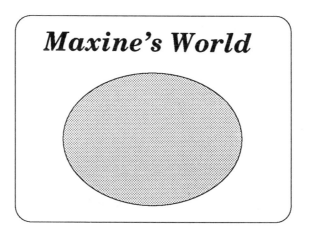

Maxine's World

"Inside every adult writer is a kid who just happened to grow up."

The publisher ...

The Profile of Africa

we wear our skin like a fine fabric
we people of colour
brown, black, tan coffeecoffee cream ebony
beautiful, strong, exotic in profile
flowering lips
silhouette obsidian planes, curves, structure
like a many-shaded mosaic
we wear our skin like a flag
we share our colour like a blanket
we cast our skin like a shadow
we wear our skin like a map
chart my beginning by my profile
chart my beginning by my colour
read the map of my heritage in
my face
my skin
the dark flash of eye
the profile of Africa.

Cashiers at the Supermarket

Cashiers never look into your eyes.
They take and trade someone else's cash
for tomatoes and cauliflower.
They see your fingers flashing nail polish, and
dirt from the field and factory
and the computer bank,
dropping, passing coins and dollars;
dollar bills, like lettuce, flutter and fall
hand to hand.
No eyes meet.
Woman at the register,
I want to see your eyes;
I want to see your youth and age.
I want to see your life in them.
Pass me my coins and cabbages
and a smile in your eyes;
or, the flicker of pain from
eight hour legs
as the register clicks and beeps
and rings up our connection
at the check-out.

Reach Out and Touch

baby girl, baby boy behind me on the bus
reach out
and touch the curly electric of my hair
your fingers dipped in the
brown skin magic of my neck
to see if it comes off
your mama
slapping hands away
hush-up of your questions
and wondering out loud
why it doesn't come off.
I turn and smile for you,
but you're already lost
in the silence and the fear that motherlove
wraps you in.
I should have sat beside you
snuggled my big warm self up close
held you while your mama juggled parcels.
then you would know it's okay.

Saskatchewan Sweetgrass Dreams

I think of you tonight
far away in some Saskatchewan dreams,
the Montreal Lake Reserve which you
sleep on this night is as close as my atlas;
I find it: growing big and small and then
big again in the fake and portable clarity
of my magnifying glass.
I see you tonight,
sharing sweetgrass in some Cree's kitchen.
The west wind brings and shares it,
and you, with me
here, so far east,
away from you, and
cradling my atlas to keep you close.

Rick Hanson: 1100 Metres High in Hinton, Alberta on March 20, 1987.

Rick Hanson crosses his last border today
leaving me,
and all of us, behind in
Halifax
St. John's
Windsor
Montreal
and everywhere;
to gripe about the snow
which keeps falling
and cold coffee;
red tape over taxes
and long lines at the cinema;
the Angus L. MacDonald toll booth,
and at the supermarket.
Rick Hansen crosses his last border today
and it's snowing in Hinton, Alberta.
I saw him on my C.B.C. Midday TV screen
and I measured his speed
against a hooting, hooting
blue and yellow VIA RAIL eastbound beside him.
It made for great TV visuals,
all that blue and yellow
and rolling wheelchair wheels
wheeling;
Hanson's tensile arms pumping;
legs wrapped and hugged tight
to his chest;
good marathon wheelchair form.
And grey Hinton, Alberta snow, falling.

In Service

In Service. I grew up hearing those words. As a little girl in my mother's kitchen, I would hear those words: *In Service.* "She went In Service." With little-girl ears where they shouldn't be, I bent to hear lady-talk. That scary, hushed, exciting lady-talk took place between my mother and women who came to see her. Tea and talk. Lady-talk.

Mama and Miss Riley went In Service. So did Mama and Aunt Lil, then Mama and Helen. Helen was the one grown-up person whose name we were allowed to say without a Miss or Aunt in front. Helen. I loved to say her name and feel her velvet hats, her tams. And she always chewed Juicy Fruit gum.

It was always the same: talk of dark and mysterious women-things, softly spoken. Lips would burble tea in cups. Eyes would roll slowly or point sharply when certain things were said and names were named. Sometimes there was talk of Mama's In Service memories and of her grandmother; a ten-year-old girl being sent in from the country, from Preston, to be In Service. I heard talk of Aunt Lil, and, sometimes talk with her. Laughing, Aunt Lil had hair like fleeting movie star dreams and Aunt Lil always included laughing in her lady-talk. But Miss Riley never did.

These conversations always seemed to carry their own colours. Sometimes it was scary, smoky black or light misty grey this lady-talk. "Children should be seen and not heard." "Keep in a child's place." I was afraid of those hard, red sentences Mama always had ready during lady-talk. I had to go where they couldn't see me. But in a small house the scary grey black mist of lady-talk can always find you.

In Service. These were sterling silver, glow-in-the-dark-and-sunlight words to me. They were like the lone brass button always at the bottom of Mama's button box when I would sneak the polish to it, to bring back the shine. The mysteries of In Service were all confused and glowing with parade dreams and uniforms marching by in a flash of things shiny and formal.

"Yes, girl, she went in service when she was 10."

"It was right after I went in service that Uncle Willy died."
"She was in service for years."

"She died in service."

My little-girl mind imagined shiny, wonderful things, never clearly defined. Not knees sore from years on hardwood floors. Not hands cracked, dry and painful, calloused and scrubworn. Not early morning walking miles into town to start the day off right with morning labours for some family. Not always going to and coming from the back door. Not "speak when you're spoken to," see and don't see, hear and don't hear, in case you anger them and they let you go. Not eating their leftovers in the kitchen alone. Not one dollar a day for back-breaking floors, walls, dishes, furniture, windows, washing, ironing, sweat-soaked labour. In Service.

"She died in service." That describes Helen. I was allowed to say her name. She was velvet tams and Juicy Fruit gum every night in Mama's kitchen. When I was little, I was allowed to stand by her and feel her tams. When I got older, she'd be there every night, watching me cry into cold dishwater.

And still the tams were there. The ruby, the emerald green, the midnight velvet blue of them glowed richly against the grey-black, soft and woolly head. Sometimes she would reach up to finger that soft glow, almost as if to make sure that lovely part of her was still there. Helen's hands against such splendid velvet were like wounds or like flags of the world of drudgery that were her days.

Helen was someone's girl, this never-married Black lady, already in middle age by the time I was old enough to know her. she was somebody's girl, but not in the romantic notion of being somebody's girlfriend. Helen was some white lady's girl; some white *family's* girl. She came to our house every night as if it was a target, an end point to her day, to sit in our kitchen with a cup of tea and to read the paper. She never took her coat off.

The lady-talk would start between Mama and Helen. It was always about Helen's lady—the woman she worked for who she called "My Missus."

Helen "lived In Service," which added to the mystique of it all. My little-girl mind imagined something with a faint glow. Not a room off the back. Not living away from your family in a house, a bed, that was never yours.

Through my window, I could see "Helen's house" not far from my own. On Sunday walks with one or other of my older sisters, seeing "Helen's house" was to see a dream, or at least a storybook page. "Helen's house" was huge and golden yellow with a fence and a yard that held what, in later, grown up years, I would know as a gazebo. But then, surely, that wonderful little in-the-yard house was where she lived, behind cool, dark green lattice. Helen's house. It was so different from my own, so squat and brown and hen-like. My house, teeming with the dozen of us. My house was where Helen fled to each night to maybe, for a little while, be a little of what my mother was. Mama, with hands on her own dishes, on her own child.

Helen had eyes that were always afraid. I would see them peek behind her tam, even as she sat and sipped her tea and waited for it all to happen every night. She waited in the wake of the dark and tiny storm of activity that hummed along after Mama, a whirlwind of shooing the creeping horde of us, of moving through clouds of flour from baking, or ironing, of putting up late supper for Daddy, of watching and listening for Daddy, and finally settling down to braid my hair and have tea and lady-talk.

Sometimes Helen would bring a shopping bag full of clothes with her to show Mama, clothes — castoff, not new — that her lady had given her. Clothes and hats. Velvet tams. Helen. Mama and Helen and lady-talk.

What did a little Black girl know, touching a velvet tam over hooded and frightened eyes? Perhaps Helen knew and feared the loneliness of her own life which circled her like the coats and tams from her shopping bag. Perhaps the secret mystery and the fear should have been hidden deep in her eyes from me, from my little-girl eyes watching Helen bring the secret of In Service each night. This world, this life, this loneliness which was all too real for her is a dark and female mystery still for me.

Helen. Helen was driven like a magnet to somebody else's kitchen, somebody else's child. Helen, with care-worn hands, handed me the future luxury of dreams, and thoughts, and "I remember Helen," and the awful mystery of In Service unravelled from the whispers of lady-talk, found now in the voice of these words.

Looking back, I know she was saving me. They all were. Helen. Mama. Miss Riley. Aunt Lil. My sisters. Known and unknown Black women. Armies of Black women in that sea of domestic service. With unlikely and un-owned addresses. Waiting for buses on prestigious street corners. Carrying back bits and remnants of that other world of In Service in shopping bags; and wearing the rest in coats and velvet tams.

I Am a Poet

I am Maxine Tynes. I am a woman. I am
Black. I am a poet. Four basic truths. None
chosen. All joyful in my life.

As a writer, I know that this creative
process was not 'chosen' by me, consciously,
as part of my life. The pursuit of the Muse,
the passion for putting life and love and
thought and feeling, into words is not
something I consciously decided to do. It is
not selected from a list of choices of being,
perhaps, a clerk, a stone mason, a nurse or
doctor, or a weaver.

It is, rather, an urge as strong, natural
and uncontrollable as an urge to laugh, to
weep, to sleep, to hold one's beloved.

To write is powerful medicine, magic,
weaponry and love.

To write poetry is the ultimate in that
power.

It is a sweet and yielding power, as well as
being an incisive and bludgeoning one.

I write from a deep, and eternal energy of
my own making and that of all of those who
have touched my life in my own time, as well
as in the distant past before my own lifetime.

When I write, I feel the hand of my
mother, Ada Maxwell Tynes; of my sisters; of
my grandmothers on both and on all sides; of
my father Joseph James Tynes; of my
brothers; and of all the men and women in
my life.

When I write, I feel the depth of my Blackness, and the spread of my Blackness through, and by, and beyond the poems and the stories of Black culture, Black life and Black womanhood that I put on paper.

My Blackness is as real to me in my poems as it is to me as I see my own Black hand move my pen and these words across the page.

My Blackness and my culture become a shared thing then with those who are and are not Black like I am. I love that.

I love to see the recognition of Black personhood in the eyes of others who share my history.

I love to see the wonder, that curious mix of fear and wonder becoming awareness of same and different and the okayness of it all in those white or other eyes. I love that.

All of that comes from writing.

All of that comes as a wonderful, ethereal return for being a poet.

That rare and wonderful state of being which I did not choose; yet, joyfully, I am.

I am Maxine Tynes.

I am a woman.

I am Black.

I am a poet.

Maxine Tynes is a poet who has lived all her life in Dartmouth, Nova Scotia. Her heritage goes back to the time of Black Loyalists in that province and Maxine has drawn heavily on that rich cultural past. Her writing is intense, personal, evocative and accessible in nature which earned her the title of Milton Acorn People's Poet of Canada for 1988. Maxine's first book, *Borrowed Beauty*, was published by Pottersfield Press in 1987. Now in its third printing, *Borrowed Beauty* has proven to be a bestselling Canadian title, reaching far beyond the usual audience for poetry. A second volume of poetry and prose, *Woman Talking Woman*, appeared in 1990. Maxine teaches English at Cole Harbour High School.

Save the World For Me is her first collection of poetry and fiction written for a young audience.

Borrowed Beauty, *Woman Talking Woman* and *Save the World For Me* are all available in book stores or directly from the publisher (Education Division, Pottersfield Press, RR 2, Porters Lake, N.S. BOJ 2SO).

A 22 minute film version of "In Service" has been produced by Red Snapper Films and is available for purchase or rental from Magic Lantern Communications Ltd., #38 - 755 Pacific Rd., Oakville, Ont. L6L 6M4 (1-800-263-1717). Nova Scotia teachers may also obtain a copy of the video for classroom use from: Nova Scotia Education Media Services, 6955 Bayers Road, Halifax, N.S. B3L 4S4